Scissor Skills
Preschool Activity Book

_____

_____

_____

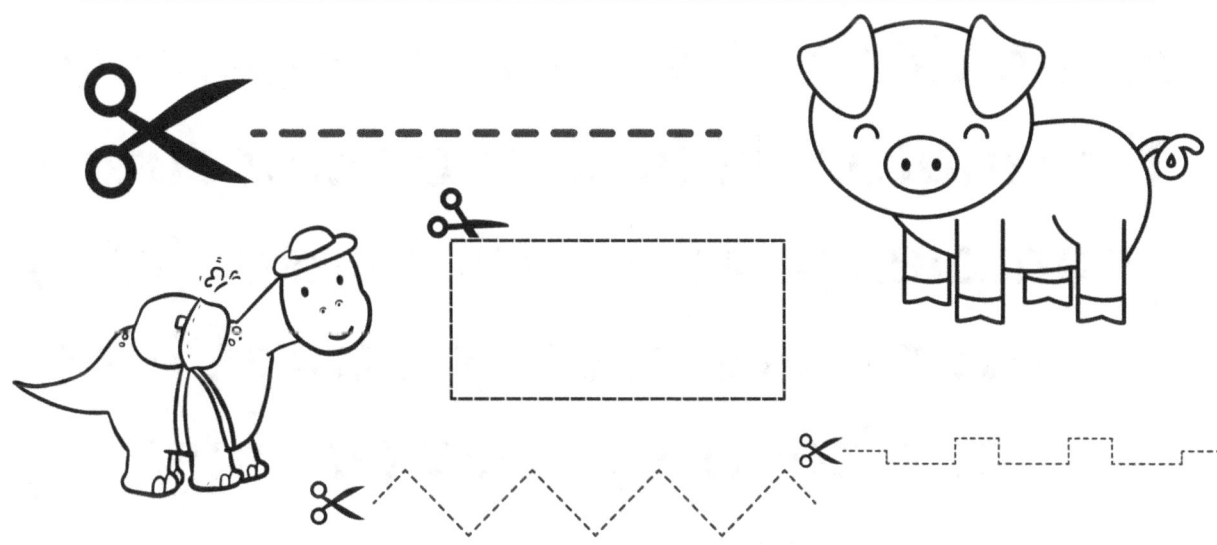

ISBN:978-1-916554-08-5

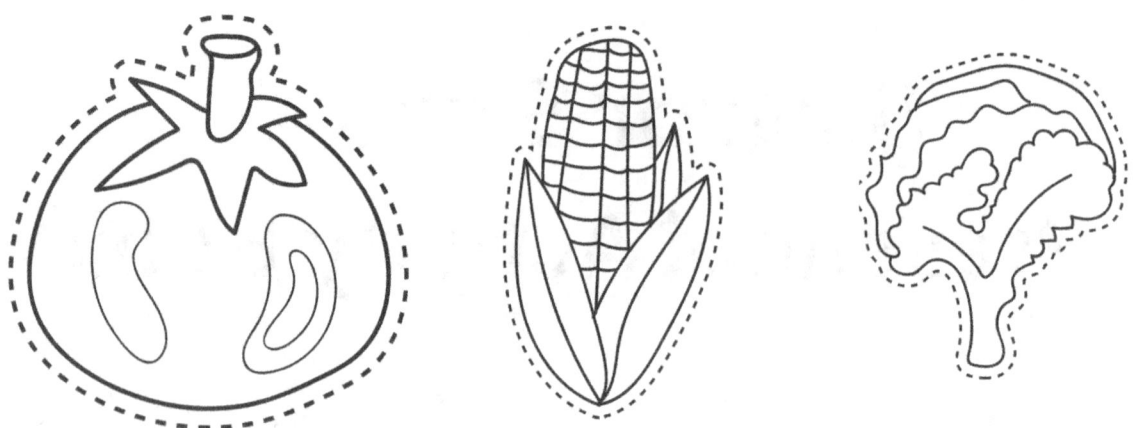

Scissor skills is something every toddler, preschooler, and kindergartener wants to start practicing As a parent, you want to do your best to keep your kids ahead. This scissors skills activity book is filled with simple scissor tasks that helps kids build their confidents and fine motor skills so they can cut out complex pictures with ease. They can even color in the pictures before or after they start cutting!

cut along straight lines

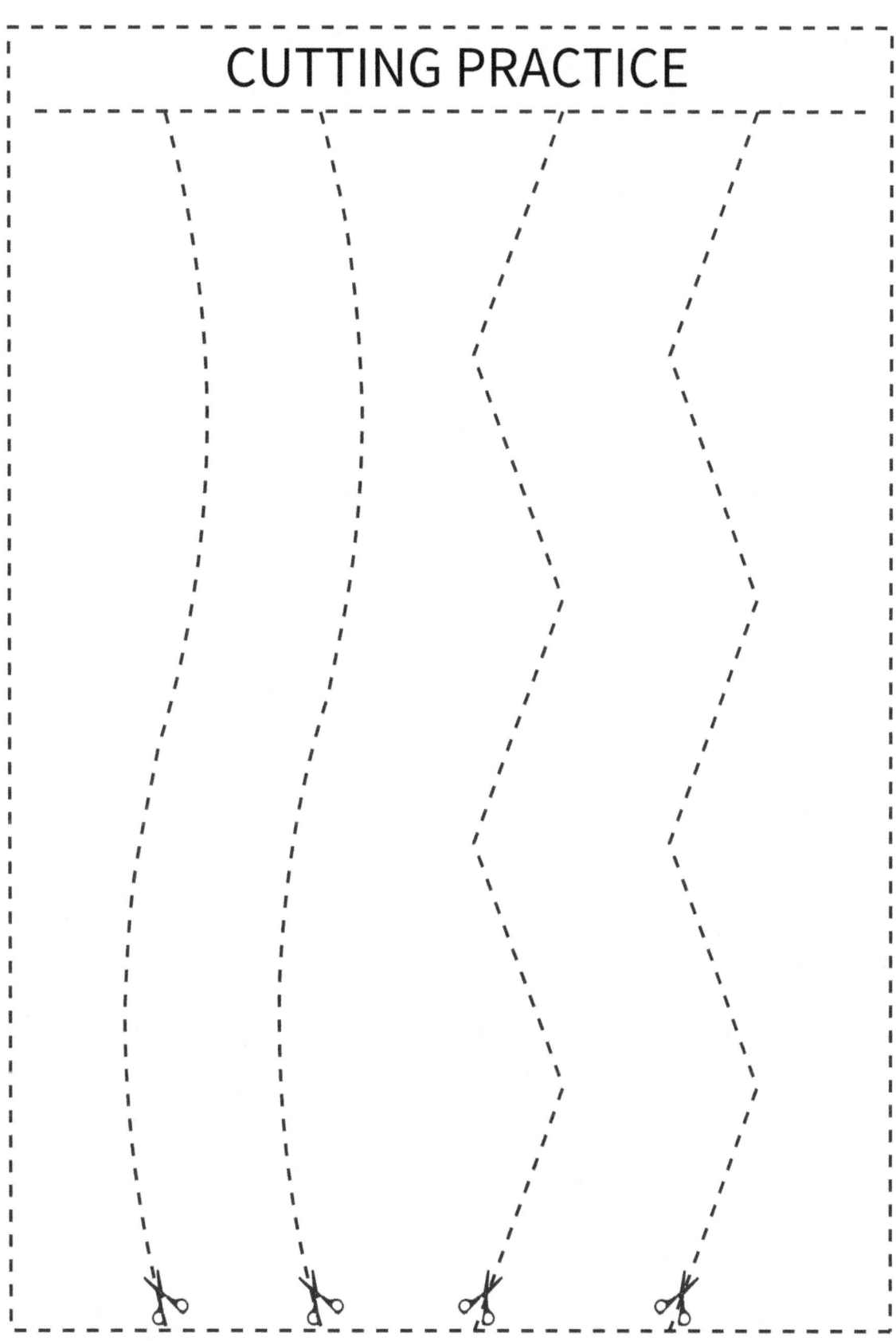

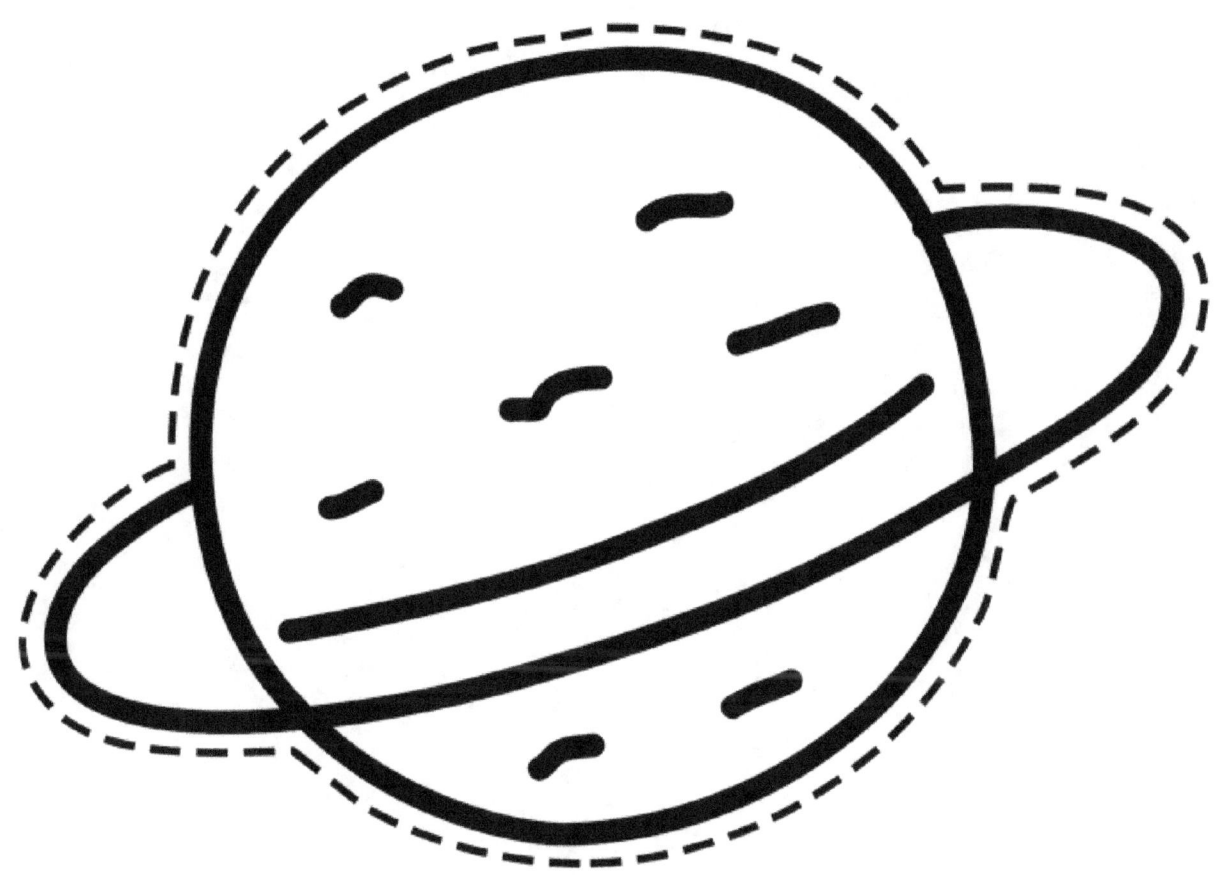

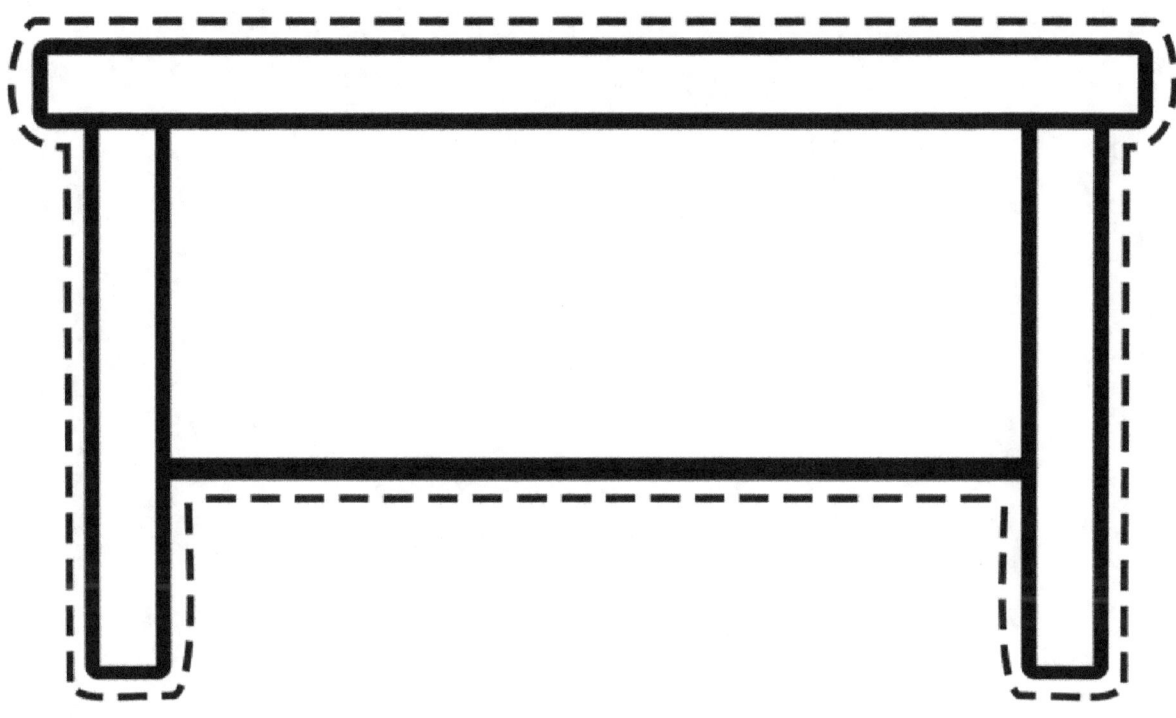

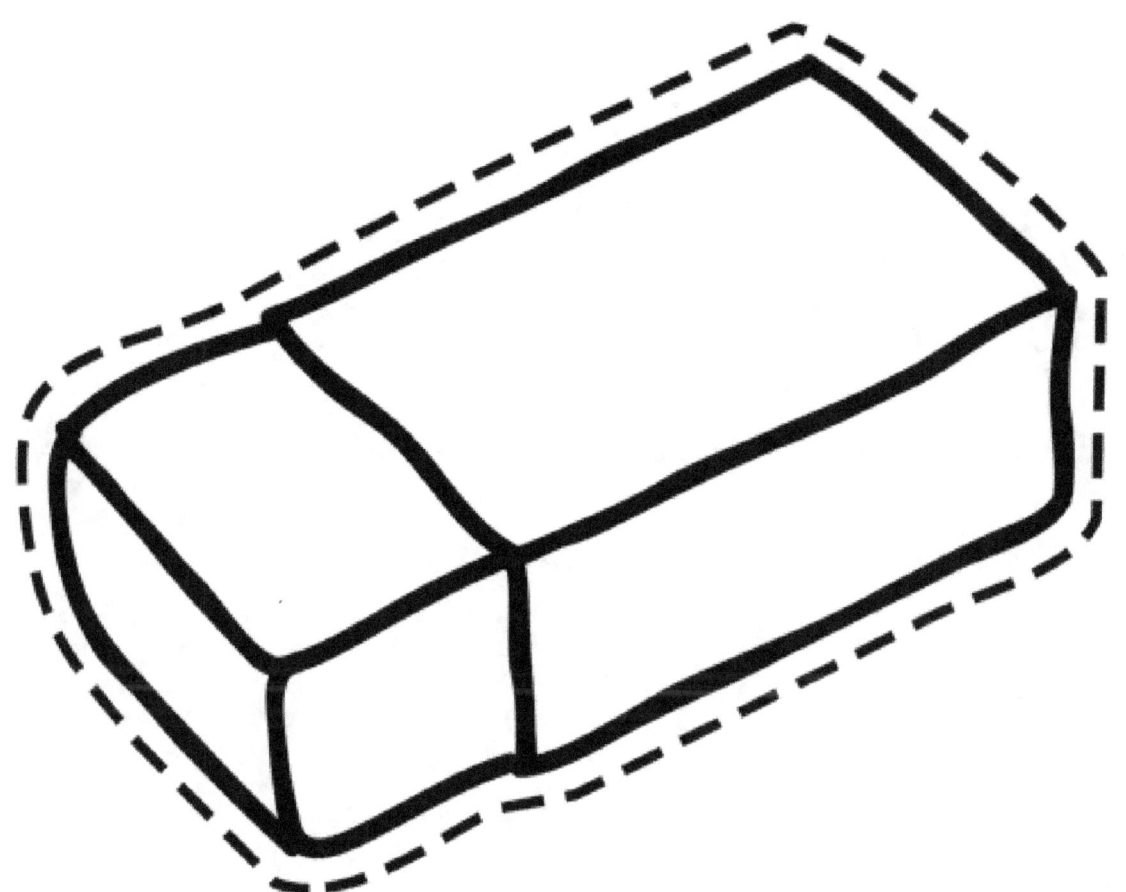

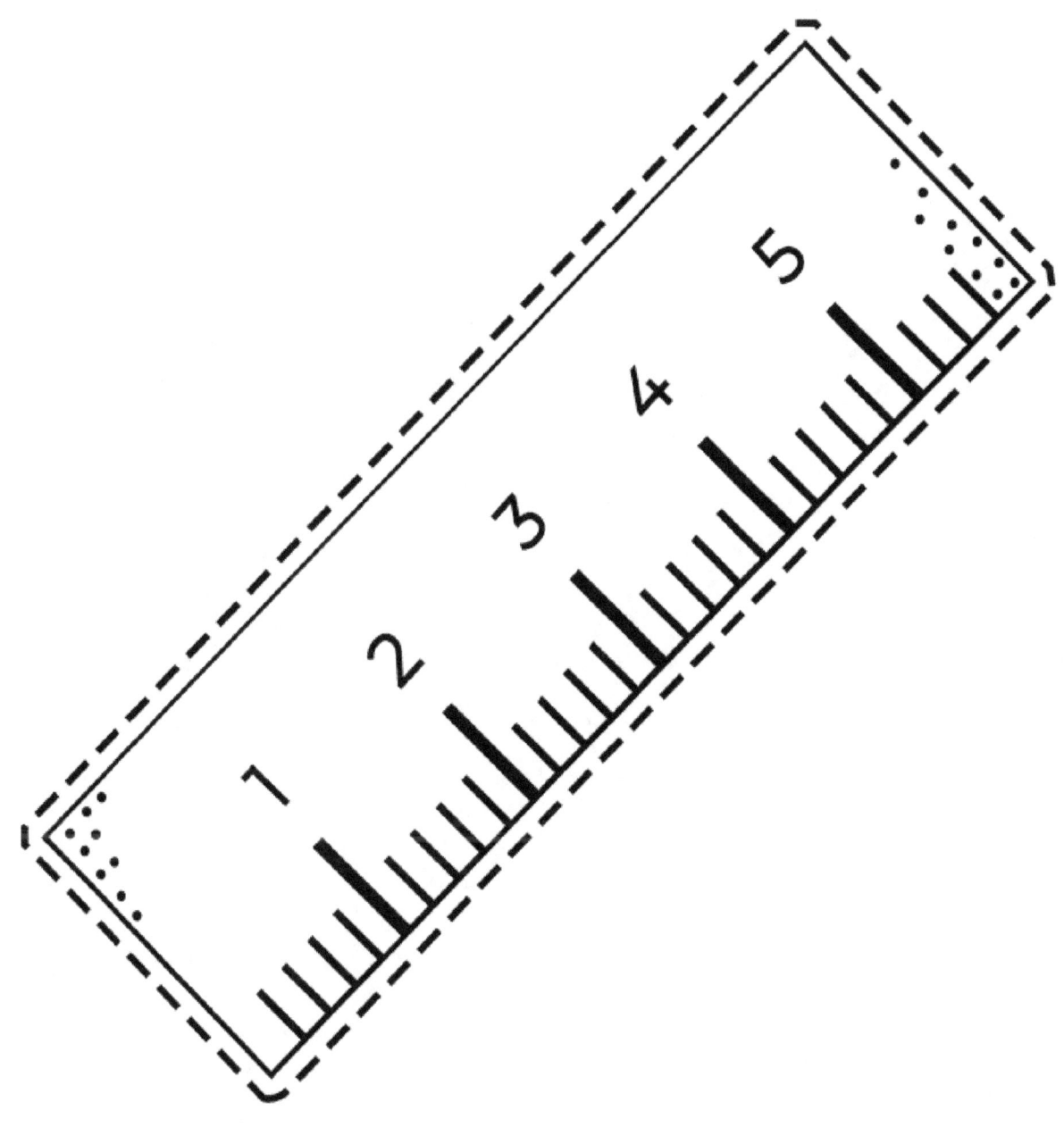

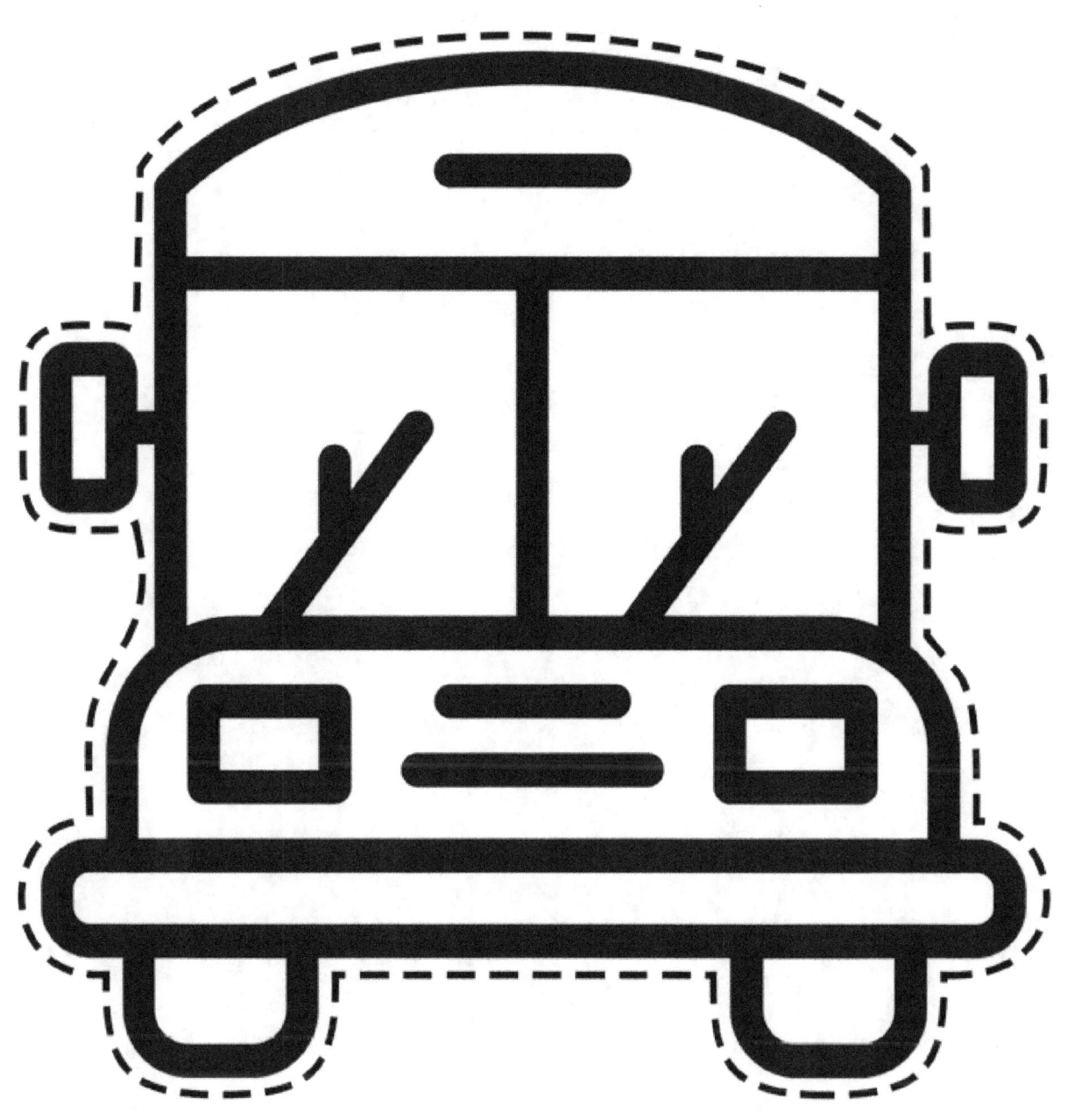

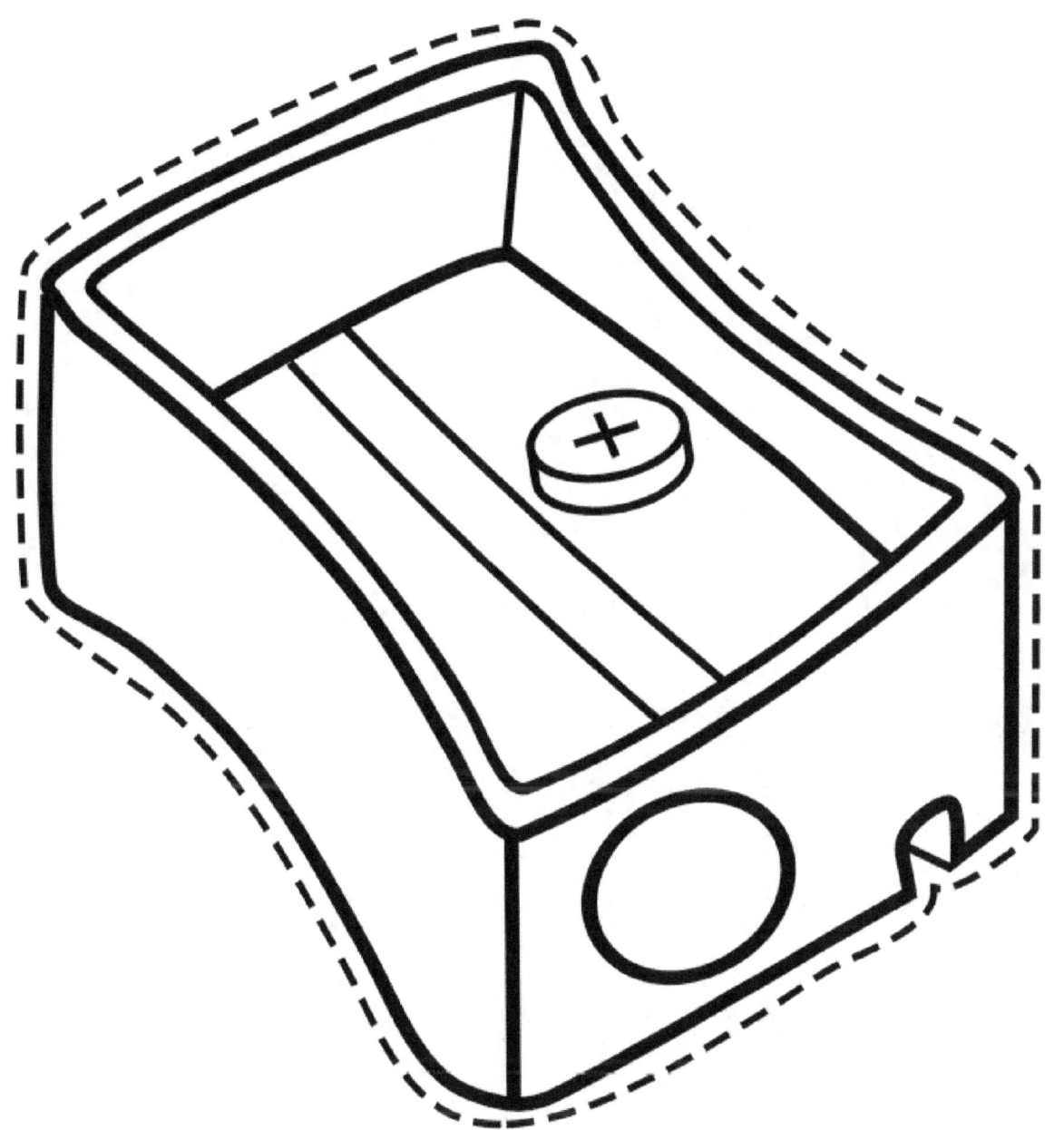

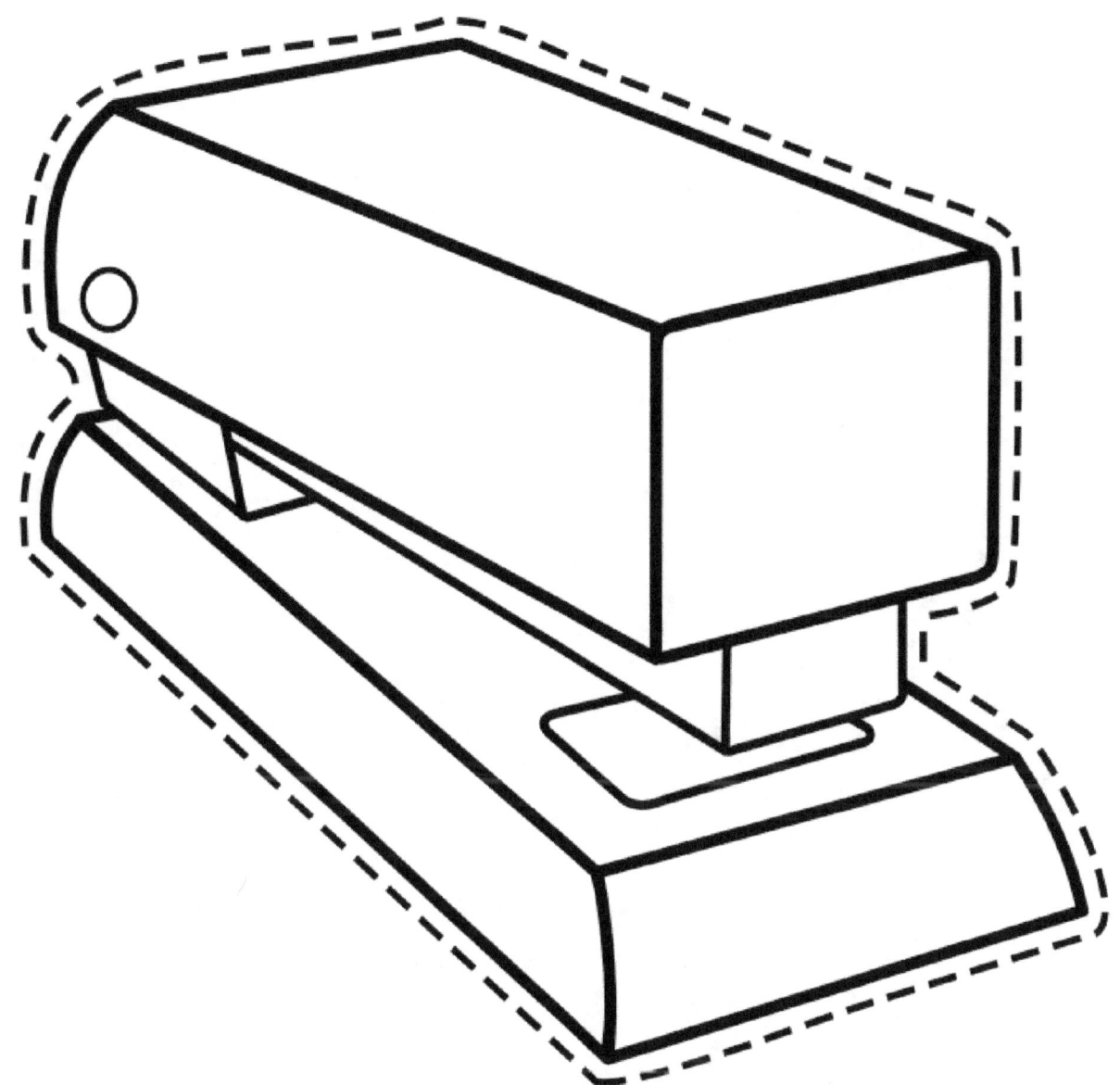

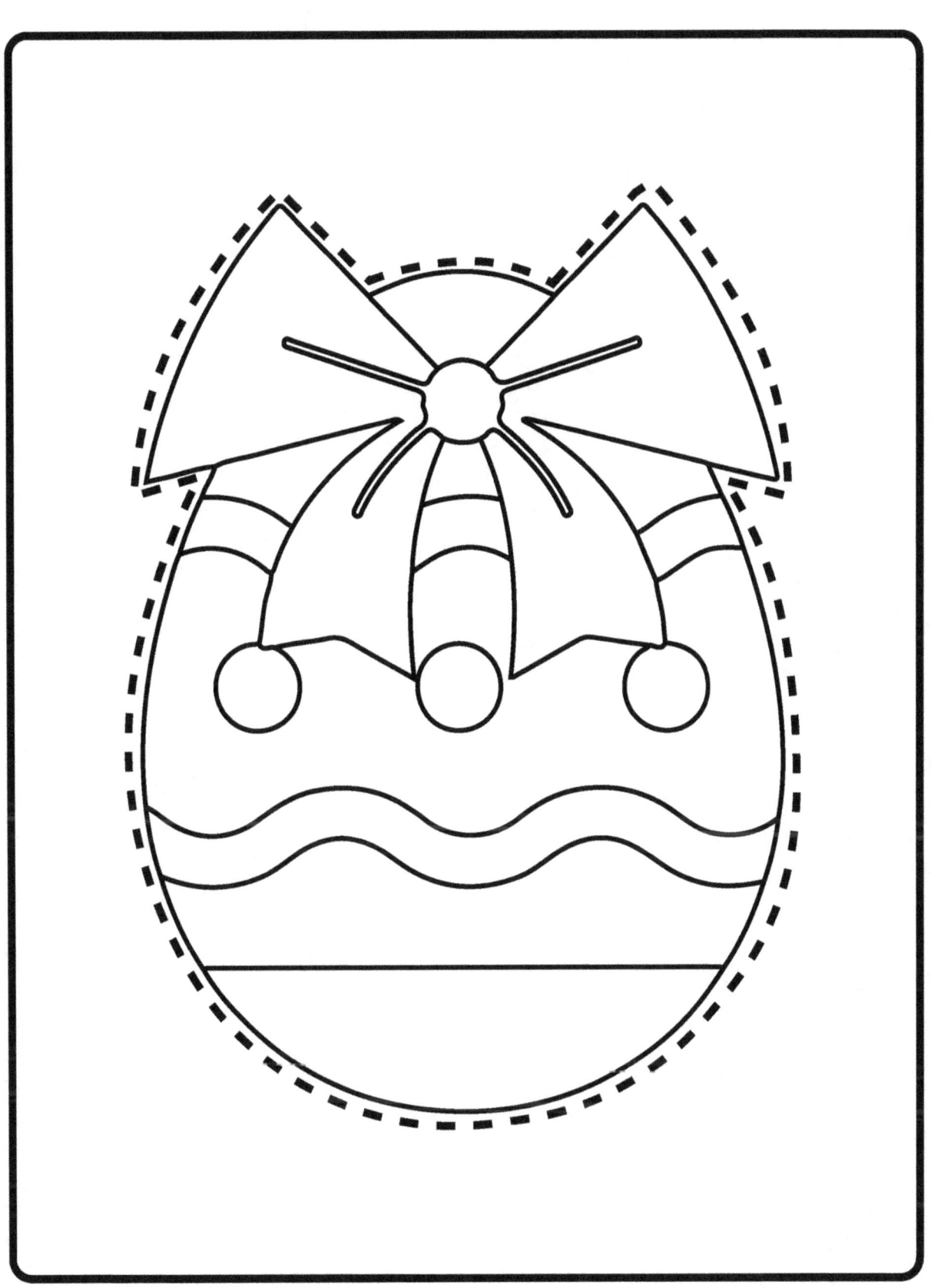

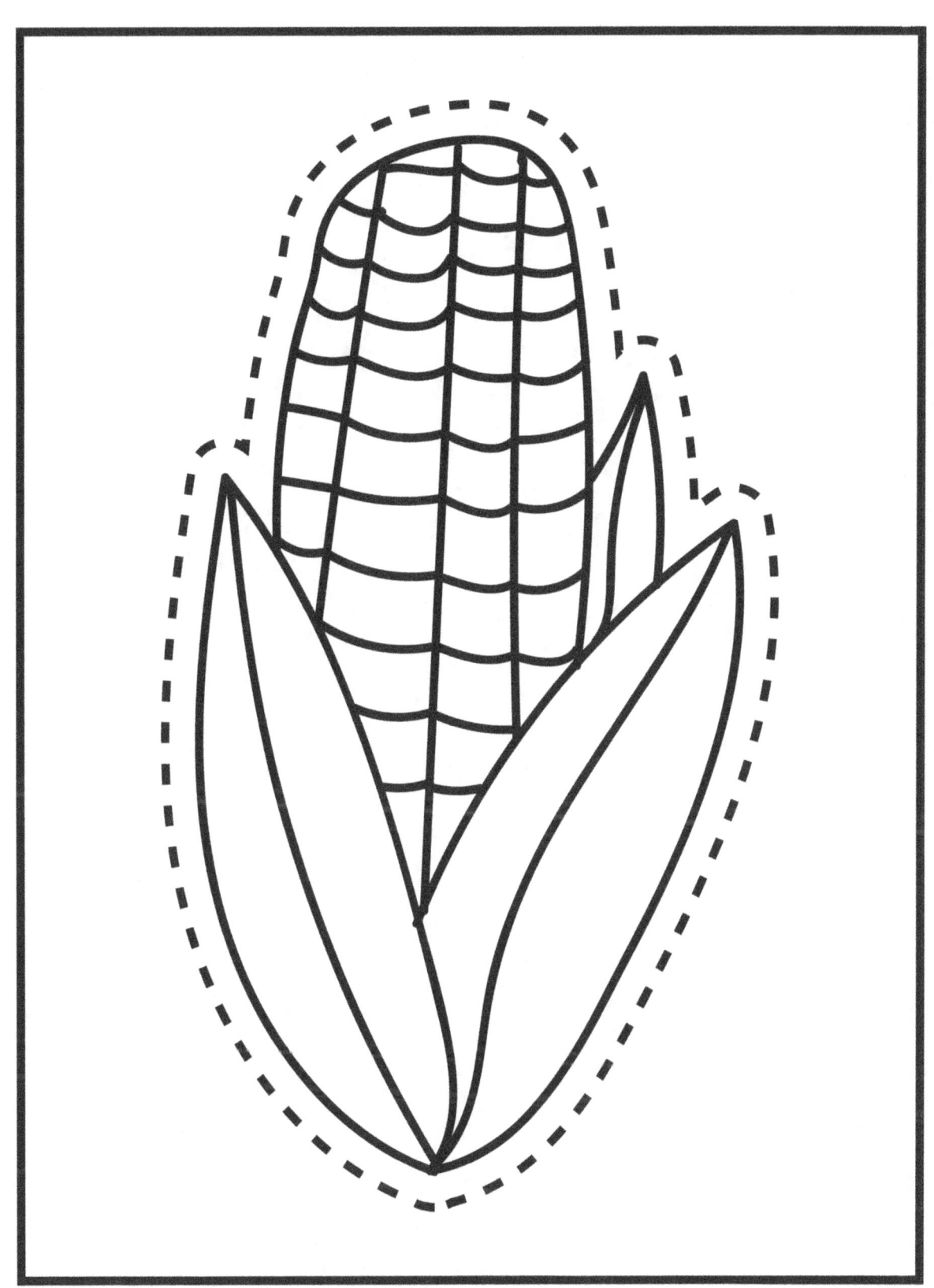

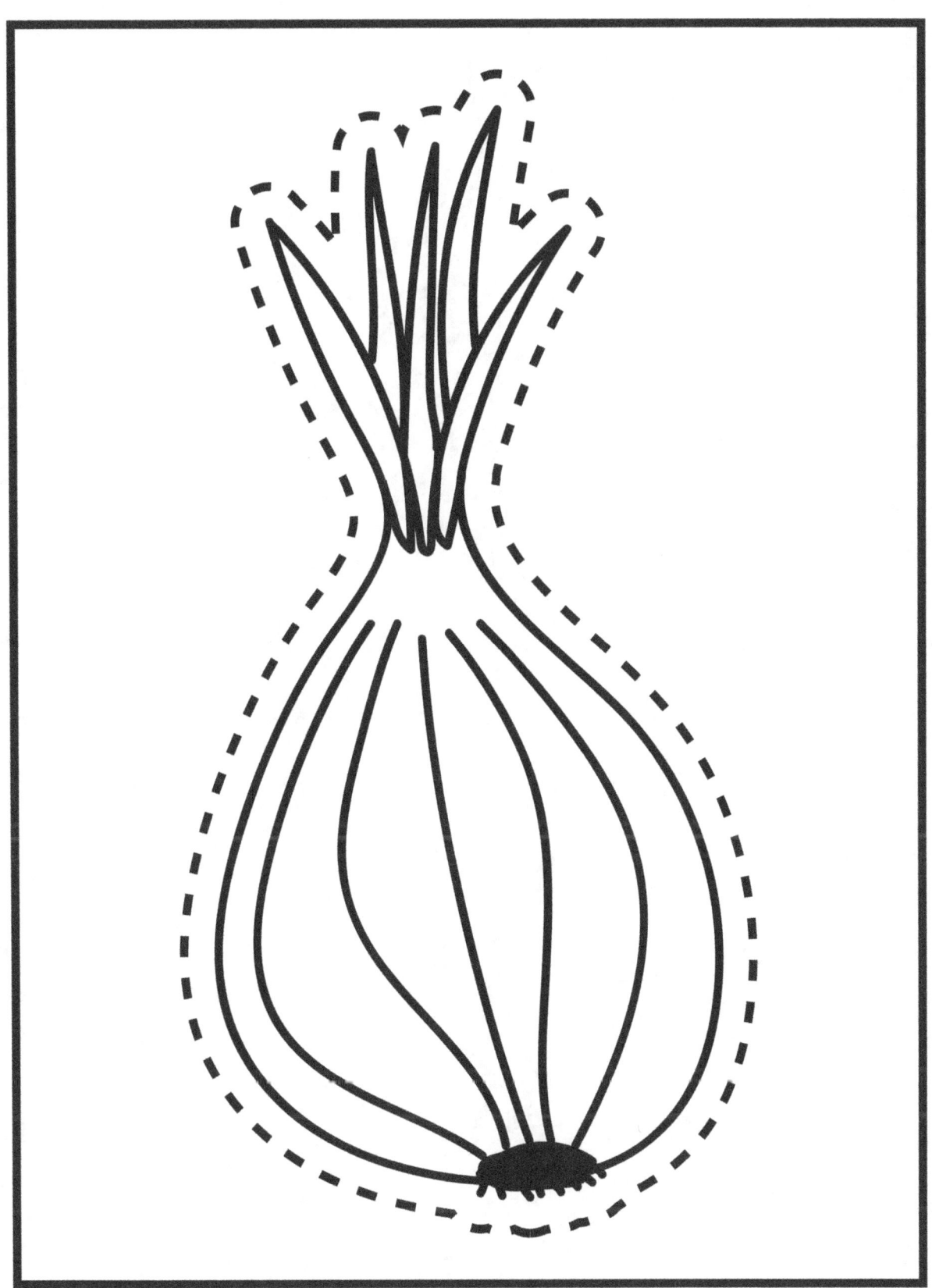

www.ingramcontent.com/pod-product-compliance
Lightning Source LLC
Chambersburg PA
CBHW081621100526
44590CB00021B/3536